PORTUGAL

UNPACKED

Susie Brooks

First published in 2014 by Wayland
Copyright © Wayland 2014

Wayland
338 Euston Road
London NW1 3BH

Wayland Australia
Level 17/207 Kent Street
Sydney, NSW 2000

Editors: Annabel Stones and Elizabeth Brent
Designer: Peter Clayman
Cover design by Matthew Kelly

Dewey number: 946.9'044-dc23

ISBN 978 0 7502 7886 7

Printed in China

10 9 8 7 6 5 4 3 2 1

Picture acknowledgements: All images and graphic elements courtesy of Shutterstock except: cover (main) © Hans-Peter Merten/Getty Images; p19 (bottom right) AFP/Getty Images; p25 (bottom right) Paul Bernhardt/Getty Images; p27 (bottom right)© Mauricio Abreu/JAI/Corbis; p29 (bottom left)© Pedro Benavente/Demotix/Corbis.

The website addresses (URLs) included in this book were valid at the time of going to press. However, it is possible that contents or addresses may change following the publication of this book. No responsibility for any such changes can be accepted by either the author or the Publisher.

Wayland is a division of Hachette Children's Books, an Hachette UK company.
www.hachette.co.uk

Contents

Portugal: Unpacked

Welcome to Portugal, the small strip of a country that's as far west in Europe as you can get! A perfect launch spot for explorers, it was once one of the most powerful places on the planet, with an empire four continents wide. Today Portugal is packed with palaces, castles, cork trees, sports fans and awesome arts and crafts. If you love beaches, come to Portugal. You'll find sunshine, surf and snow here. So let's get unpacking!

Fact File

Area: 92,090km^2
Population: 10,799,270 (July 2013 est.)
Capital city: Lisbon
Land Borders: 1,214km with Spain
Currency: The Euro

Flag:

Portugal

Useful Phrases

Olá/Bom dia – Hello (informal/formal)
Tchau! – Bye!
Como estás? – How are you?
Muito bem – Very well
Obrigado/a – Thank you (if you're a boy/girl)
Por favor – Please
Meu nome é – My name is
Fala inglês? – Do you speak English?
Onde é o banheiro? – Where is the toilet?
Vamos! – Let's go!

Portuguese isn't just spoken in Portugal.

It's also the official language of Brazil, Cape Verde, Angola, Guinea Bissau, Mozambique, Principe, Sao Tome and Equatorial Guinea. People in Goa (India), Macao and East Timor use it too!

Fishing is big business here. The Portuguese eat more seafood per person than any other nation in Europe!

Surfers love Portugal for its year-round swell. In 2013, Garrett McNamara claimed to have caught a record 30.5-metre wave off the coast at Nazaré!

Small Country, Big Story

Calling all time travellers - if you want a real adventure, go back into Portugal's past! You can follow in the footsteps of Celts, Romans, Visigoths and Moors here, not to mention brave explorers, super-rich monarchs and tough dictators. Portugal ruled the first global empire in history, and the longest one modern Europe has ever seen. It may be a small country, but its story is certainly huge!

At the ruins of Conimbriga you can step right back to Roman times!

The Old Days

The Romans had a hard time conquering Portugal – it took them nearly 200 years! A Celtic leader called Viriatus did a lot to stop them, until eventually they killed him in his sleep. By 19BCE, the Celts were out and the Romans ruled until the 400s. That's when Germanic tribes, and later North African Moors, invaded. You don't have to look far to find forts, art and other traces from these times.

Check out Portugal's explorers on the Monument to the Discoveries in Lisbon.

NO WAY!

Between 1910 and 1926, Portugal had 45 governments, 20 military takeovers and 12 presidents!

Age of Discovery

There was excitement in the 1400s, when Portuguese explorers took to the seas. They became the first Europeans to cross the equator, round Africa's Cape of Good Hope, sail east to India and set foot in South America. They claimed land wherever they went and launched an empire that would last for more than 500 years. In the 1500s, Portugal's monarchy was the richest in Europe!

The Republic

Portugal became a republic in the early 1900s. A prime minister called Salazar took control in 1932, ruling with an iron fist until he died in 1970. By then, people were poor and unhappy, and wars were tearing Portugal's colonies apart. On 25 April 1974, army rebels stormed the streets and overthrew the leadership. To celebrate, soldiers put flowers in their gun barrels and the Carnation Revolution got its name!

Lisbon's 25 April Bridge is named after the date of the Revolution.

Let's Play!

It's sunny for 300 days of the year in parts of Portugal, so no wonder people like to get outside and play! Open-air activities are the name of the game here for locals and visitors alike. From water skiing, sailing and surfing to climbing, tennis and athletics - sports fans really are spoilt for choice. And if you're keen to kick a ball around, a football-mad friend won't be hard to find!

NO WAY!

Cristiano Ronaldo owns cars by Lamborghini, Ferrari, Aston Martin, Rolls-Royce, Bentley, Mercedes-Benz, Porsche, Maserati, BMW ...and more!

Cristiano Ronaldo takes a kick.

Football Fever

A word of warning when a football match is on – don't get in the way of the TV! The Portuguese are fanatical supporters, especially when their local team is playing. Clubs like Porto and Benfica have massive followings and are big winners in the Portuguese league. As for the national team, with stars such as Cristiano Ronaldo they ooze talent, even if they're yet to win a major title.

Whirling Wheels

Portuguese motorists like to go fast – especially on their racing circuits. A whole host of top competitions happen here, including World Superbike and Touring Car championships. Off-track racing is popular too, with the famous Rally de Portugal roaring through Lisbon and the Algarve. If cycling's more your thing, visit for the Volta a Portugal or just hit the hills and pedal!

The Rally de Portugal is an exhilarating three-day race!

A windsurfer skims across the clear blue sea of the Algarve.

Sunshine Sports

The Algarve, in southern Portugal, is one of the most popular golfing spots in Europe. In fact, it's famous worldwide. You can thank the weather for that – oh, and the Brits who introduced the sport! Some of the best courses are right on the coast with brilliant views. If you'd rather be in the water than looking at it, kitesurfing, wakeboarding and scuba diving are just a few other things you can try.

Holiday Hotspots

A record 7.7 million foreigners visited Portugal in 2012 - that's quite a lot for a country of less than 11 million people! We all know about the sun-drenched sandy beaches, bustling cities, and pretty villages, but there are plenty of other highlights too...

The Portuguese royal family used to summer at Sintra – a place of palaces, castles and parks. At the Quinta da Regaleira you can get lost in caves and tunnels, reached by a spiral staircase in a well.

In Evora's 'Chapel of Bones', a sign at the entrance reads: 'We, the bones that are here, await yours...' Inside, the walls are covered with the skeletons and skulls of about 5,000 monks!

Aveiro is the Venice of Portugal – a busy old city, criss-crossed by canals. Tourists can ride in brightly coloured *moliceiros*, traditionally seaweed-trawling boats.

In 1190, a 70-year-old warrior monk (and his men) defended the city of Tomar against Moorish invaders. Visit the wondrous Knights Templar Castle to see what all the fuss was about.

Fancy sleeping in a palace, castle, convent, monastery or magnificent manor house? Portugal's *pousadas* let you do just that! The buildings have been converted into hotels.

If you like fairytale villages, head to Monsaraz or Óbidos. Built within medieval castle walls, their whitewashed houses are postcard-perfect. Climb up to the battlements for cool views.

Sun, Sand and Serras

Portugal clings to the edge of Spain and is dwarfed by its six-times-bigger neighbour. Still, there's plenty of landscape to explore here, from mountains and forests to beaches, wetlands and plains. It's one of Europe's warmest countries, though you'll need a raincoat in the cooler, wetter north. In the mountains you can shiver at a wintry -20°C - or sizzle up to 40°C in the southern summer!

Starry Heights

Serra da Estrela means 'Mountain Range of the Star', and it's home to mainland Portugal's highest peak, Torre. Unusually, you can drive right up it, and the summit (1,993m) is marked in the middle of a roundabout! There's a ski resort nearby, and while you're up there try the gooey sheep's cheese that's named after the range. If you're wondering what to eat it on, visit the local Bread Museum for ideas!

Blue sky and fresh snow are a popular combination for skiers!

Seaside Sights

Portugal's coastline is 1,793km long – that's further than from Lisbon to London! Huge stretches of the west are wild and unspoilt, while beaches in the south attract sun-seeking crowds. Look out for the Boca do Infierno (Hell's Mouth) – a rocky chasm where the sea really roars. Windswept Cabo Sao Vicente is the most south-westerly point of mainland Europe, once thought to be the end of the world.

The lighthouse at Cabo Sao Vicente is one of the brightest in Europe!

Winds and dry weather make fires like this very difficult to control.

Summer Scorchers

In the dry summer months, things can get hot – very hot – in parts of Portugal. Forests of pine, eucalyptus and oak cover nearly 40% of the country, and wildfires break out here every year. You may find ash falling on your head as it often drifts into towns – it can even close major roads. A team of heroic volunteers, called the *Bombeiros Voluntários*, risk their lives to fight the flames.

Island Magic

Way back in 1418, a group of Portuguese sailors were blown off course in the Atlantic. The good news was they bumped into a tiny island, which later led them to a bigger one - Madeira! Around 1427, the Portuguese also discovered the Azores. Both archipelagos are now popular stop-offs for cruise ships, and a paradise for people who love exotic birds and plants.

Madeira Mountain

Known as 'God's floating garden' thanks to its lush landscape, Madeira is the peak of a mountain range rising 6.5km from the seabed! You can peer over the world's second-highest cliff face here, and see terraced hillsides, planted with vines and bananas. Follow criss-crossing *levadas* (irrigation channels) to explore the island. A wicker toboggan ride from Monte to Funchal is not to be missed.

You'll find these quirky thatched houses in the town of Santana, Madeira.

Adore the Azores

If you're cruising from Europe to America, the Azores are a great place to stop. These nine unspoilt islands are a treasure trove of volcanic craters, black-sand beaches, palaces, gardens, windmills, waterfalls, hot springs, geysers and more. At the thermal town of Furnas, locals bury casserole dishes in the ground and cook using the Earth's heat! Europe's oldest tea estate is found here too.

The volcanic landscape around Furnas is hot underground – ideal for cooking pits!

NO WAY!

Madeira's wicker toboggans can zoom downhill at nearly 50km/hour. The men who steer them use their feet as brakes!

Birdy Berlengas

Pirates, shipwrecks, buried treasure – the Berlengas have seen it all! These tiny islands, close to the coast north of Lisbon, are one of Portugal's best-kept secrets. In the 1500s, monks set up a monastery here to help sailors in distress. It was later replaced by a fort that's now a hostel. Stay here while you enjoy the crystal-clear waters, white sands and more birds and fish than people.

The fort was completed in 1656 as a defence against pirates and invaders.

Charismatic Cities

There's a saying in Portugal that goes like this: 'Coimbra sings, Braga prays, Porto works and Lisbon shows off'! These are just four of the country's great cities, which all have characters of their own. The biggest cities are by the coast, often acting as major ports. About two-thirds of the population live in urban areas - a change from 50 years ago, when most Portuguese were rural folk.

NO WAY!

Lisbon's Vasco da Gama bridge is the longest in Europe (17.2km). When it opened, 16,000 people had lunch on it, at a table 5km long!

Porto's historic centre is now a World Heritage Site.

Important Porto

Porto is Portugal's second-largest city, and a rival to Lisbon if you ask its nearly 2 million residents! It's a colourful maze of a place, with old shops and alleys, bell towers, iconic bridges, modern arts, concert halls, and wine caves with barrels the size of lorries. Many people here have moved to shiny seaside suburbs, while the old city centre has a tumbledown charm.

Clever Coimbra

For over 100 years in the Middle Ages, Coimbra was Portugal's capital. Now it's a place where history lives on, with ancient lanes, medieval churches and an 18th-century library where bats eat bugs that would ruin the books! The university, founded in 1290, is one of the oldest in the world. Graduating students hold big parties and burn coloured ribbons that were attached to their robes.

Lively Lisbon

Lisbon is Europe's second-oldest capital after Athens – it's even older than Rome! Even so, it feels lively and modern, with about 3 million people living here. There's a lot to take in, including the ancient Belém Tower, Jerónimos monastery, St George's Castle and an impressive Oceanarium. If your feet get weary of the cobbled streets, you can hop on a vintage tram to explore.

Lisbon is built on seven hills, so take some comfy shoes!

More than 20,000 students go to Coimbra University.

Made in Portugal

What's made in Portugal? Lots! Chugging out of the country's ports you'll find cars, cameras, shoes, fuels, T-shirts, toilet paper… the list goes on! Exports are important for the country's economy, and foreign companies are taking advantage of the nation's skilled workforce and hi-tech expertise.

Motoring Away

At the VW AutoEuropa factory 112,550 cars, each made up of over 3,500 parts, are built in a single year. Vehicle manufacturing is big in Portugal and you'll also find bikes, plane seats, cruise ships, and even spacecraft components, coming hot off the press for global buyers!

The VW Scirocco is made in Portugal for export.

Bright Sparks

The ICT sector employs about 79,000 people and makes billions of euros a year. The world's first GPS with aerial photos was created here, as well as the first pre-paid mobile phone card. If you travel on the London Underground, you're using Portuguese technology too.

No more getting lost, thanks to the Portuguese ICT industry.

Wares to Wear

For the second-most expensive shoes after Italy, look to Portugal! Their luxury leather goods are well known. Textiles and clothing make up 12% of all exports from the country. Sales reps travel non-stop to get the best deals abroad, and mills churn out miles of fabric daily.

NO WAY!

Rumour has it that Simon Cowell is a fan of Renova Black toilet tissue, while Beyoncé demands the red version in her dressing room!

The Write Stuff

Portugal's pulp and paper industry is one of the biggest in Europe, accounting for around 60% of office paper exports to the rest of the world. It's something to write home about – and so is the loo paper. Innovative Portuguese brand Renova sells in more than 60 countries!

Renova stocks are piled high to keep up with demand!

Country Corkers

If you like the idea of stepping back in time, head to the Portuguese countryside! Many hamlets and villages feel like they haven't changed for centuries, but that doesn't stop about a third of the population wanting to live here. Portugal has the highest rate of rural living in western Europe, and even though farming can be a tough life, many people who are fed up with cities are returning to the land.

Traditional stone houses cling to the hillside at Piódão.

North and South

It's one thing in the north and another in the south in Portugal. Northern farmers are more likely to plant cabbages, corn and potatoes and live in two-storey houses, where animals were once kept on the ground floor. In the south, Moorish-style villages are whitewashed with flat roofs and blue-trimmed windows and doors. Citrus fruits, figs and olives grow well in these sunnier parts.

Bouncy Bark

No prizes for guessing what you get from the cork oak tree. Its soft, springy bark is turned into...um... cork! Portugal is the world's largest producer of cork products. Most come from the Alentejo, a hot plain in the centre-south that's also big on wheat. Foresters strip the trees every 10 years – the time it takes for the bark to grow back. This does no harm; a cork oak can live to be 250!

NO WAY!

Many port wineries, or *quintas*, have English names, as in fact it was British merchants in Portugal who made the drink famous!

You can tell a newly stripped cork tree by its brightly coloured trunk.

Great Grapes

Port comes from near Porto, of course! More specifically, it's produced in the Douro Valley, the world's first marked wine area and now a World Heritage site. Grapes have been growing here for more than 2,000 years, and the soil and climate are perfect. September is harvesting season – you can go and help pick if you like. Stomping on grapes to crush them is a fun tradition to join in too!

Visitors can cruise down the Douro River and sip port as they go!

Wild Times

Rabbits, hares, badgers and bats are common things to see in Portugal. You'll also find a fair few creepy crawlies and reptiles scuttling around. It's a birdwatcher's dream with around 600 species, and a treat for flower fans too...

Darting up walls and trees or under rocks... you'll see plenty of lizards running away from you! They're shy creatures and can even drop their tail off if they're really scared.

Greater flamingos wade in wetlands in big pink flocks. They honk like geese and get their quirky colouring from the shrimps they eat.

Portuguese water dogs are rare, shaggy, webbed-footed creatures. They used to help fishermen round up fish into their nets. Now people keep them as pets, including US President Barack Obama!

Portugal's wild orchids have some descriptive names, like champagne, bumble-bee, mirror and naked man! They're protected by law, so no picking.

Dinosaurs died out 65 million years ago. If you want to see creatures more than 400 million years old, check out Portugal's fossil trilobites – they're a bit like giant woodlice!

Talk about a greedy pig, the wild boar eats almost anything that will fit in its mouth! This hairy porker runs fast, swims well and has an excellent sense of smell.

Are you brave enough to dive with sharks? Then head to the Azores. Blue sharks are curious and like to swim up close. Makos, the fastest sharks, will come and go in a flash.

Make Yourself at Home

Don't be surprised if you get a hero's welcome here - the Portuguese love children! Life is all about family, and when grown-ups stay up late, the kids often get to, too. You'll find families living together, working together and out and about together. No one's too bothered about being on time - but they're sticklers for good manners, so watch your *por favors*!

Portuguese children learn English at primary school.

School Days

Children may have their freedom in Portugal, but there's no getting out of school! It's compulsory for everyone aged 6 to 15. Most lessons run from 9am to 3.30pm, though some pupils go to breakfast or after-school clubs. There's a long lunch break – and an even longer summer holiday! It lasts for 10 weeks, and many children spend time with their grandparents while their parents work.

Portugal's a great place for family outings to the beach!

Being Portuguese

The Portuguese prefer not to be compared to their Spanish neighbours. After all, they have their own language, culture and traditions. Families revel in local arts, crafts, concerts and café chatter, not to mention shopping malls, where they can chill out in the summer heat! People dress stylishly, both for work and play. If you see them wearing peasant clothes, it's probably a special occasion.

Bands parade at a *romaria*, a type of religious festival or pilgrimage.

Pray and Play

Look out in Porto on the night of 23 June. People dance through the streets, hitting each other on the head with plastic hammers! This is St John's Eve, one of many Christian festivals, or *festas*. Most Portuguese are Roman Catholic, but they are free to choose any religion. There are still some descendents of the Marranos – Jews who kept their faith secret in the days when only Catholicism was allowed.

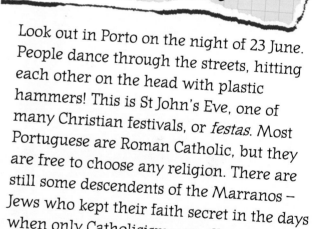

Surf 'n' Turf

Are you a fussy eater, or do you have daring tastes? Either way, you won't go hungry in Portugal. It's a place where food matters, and every region has its own local treats on the menu. The Portuguese love talking about food almost as much as they love eating it, so if in doubt just say 'YUM'!

Seafood staples

It might make your mouth water, or your toes curl... *bacalhau* is a love-hate dish. This dried, salted cod is served around the country in all kinds of ways – some say there are more than 1,000 recipes! *Caldeirada* is another fishy feast, with cod, sardines, haddock, tuna, mackerel (or whatever a fishermen can catch) cooked in a stew. It's juicy, so slurp it up with some crusty bread.

In Portugal you can eat cod a different way every day!

Meat menu

For meat lovers, *cozido à portuguesa* might be tempting. It's a chunky stew of beef shin, pork (sometimes trotters and ears!), smoked or blood sausage and vegetables. If surf 'n' turf is more your thing, try *porco à alentejana* – pork and clams in wine and coriander. Garlicky grilled meats and a boggling choice of hams are tasty too. Pick up a bottle of popular *piri piri* sauce to add some spice!

Pork with clams is typical of the Alentejo region.

NO WAY!

Some traditional dishes use pig or chicken blood as a base - look out for the words *sarrabulho* and *cabidela*.

Sweet Stuff

Prepare to pile on the pounds with Portuguese puddings. For a start, they claim to make the world's best custard tarts, or *pastéis de nata*. Fans of rice pudding can drool over *arroz doce* – it's sticky and citrus flavoured, with a fancy cinnamon pattern on the top. If you're in a bakery, try ordering pastries with names like *papos de anjo* (angel's double-chins) and *barriga de freiras* (nuns' belly)!

Try a star-topped rice pudding at Christmas!

Custard tarts are a Portuguese treasure.

27

Creative Culture

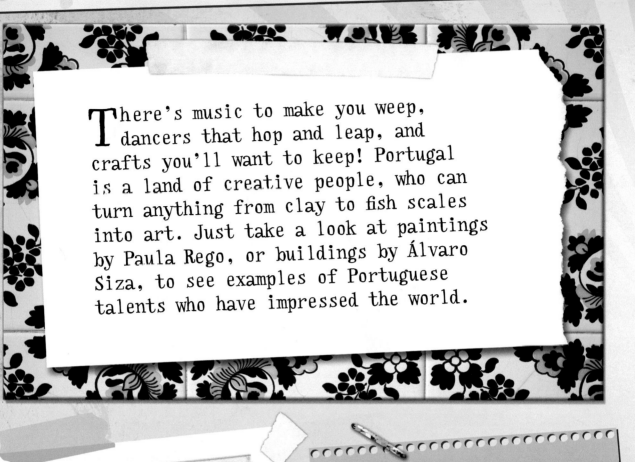

There's music to make you weep, dancers that hop and leap, and crafts you'll want to keep! Portugal is a land of creative people, who can turn anything from clay to fish scales into art. Just take a look at paintings by Paula Rego, or buildings by Álvaro Siza, to see examples of Portuguese talents who have impressed the world.

Tile Style

Tiles aren't just for kitchens – in Portugal they decorate whole houses! Moorish *azulejos* brighten up walls with anything from abstract patterns to historic battle scenes. You can check out tiles by contemporary artists in many of Lisbon's metro stations.

 Blue is a popular colour for *azulejos*.

Nautical Walls

Why would you carve seaweed, ropes, buoys and anchors on your buildings? To celebrate the great seafaring age, of course! Manueline architecture is a flashy 16th-century style that shows off Portugal's triumphant past.

Manueline is named after King Manuel I, who reigned from 1495–1521.

Sad Songs

It's not the cheeriest music, but the Portuguese go mad for fado. Think of a sad, kind of homesick sound, with a singer dressed in black and a 12-stringed guitar that players pluck with their fingertips (ouch). Coimbra and Lisbon both have their own styles of fado.

Dizzy Dance

Hold your arms in the air and twirl, hop and skip! The Vira, a Portuguese folk dance, is fast-paced and fun. You might see it on a village dance floor, or *terreiro*.

Dancers perform the Vira in traditional dress.

A fado singer is called a fadista.

More Information

Websites

http://www.lonelyplanet.com/portugal
http://www.roughguides.com/destinations/europe/portugal/
All you need to prepare for a trip to Portugal.

http://www.worldtravelguide.net/portugal
A travel site with plenty of background info.

http://kids.nationalgeographic.co.uk/kids/places/find/portugal/
Facts and photos from the National Geographic.

http://www.golisbon.com/
Packed with information about Portugal's capital city.

http://www.portugal.net/
A guide to Portugal past and present.

http://www.theportugalnews.com/
The latest news and headlines in Portugal.

http://portugal-lol.com/
Everything fun in Portugal for kids!

http://www.bbc.co.uk/news/world-europe-17758217
A country profile by the BBC.

https://www.cia.gov/library/publications/the-world-factbook/geos/po.html
The CIA World Factbook page, with up-to-date info and statistics.

Apps

Google Earth by Google, inc
Explore Portugal (and the rest of the world) from the sky – for free!

The World by National Geographic
Tour the whole world with interactive maps, facts and photos.

Portugal Travel Guide by Triposo
Up to-date city guides for Lisbon, Porto, Faro and many other hotspots.

Learn Portuguese – MindSnacks by MindSnacks
A fun and free way to learn Portuguese!

Cristiano Ronaldo Freestyle Soccer by Digital Artists Entertainment
Pull off Ronaldo's kicks and tricks in an action-packed game!

Clips

http://vimeo.com/60564362
A promotional video from the National Geographic Channel.

http://www.bbc.co.uk/languages/portuguese/talk/
A series of videos to help you learn to speak Portuguese.

http://video.nationalgeographic.com/video/music/genre-wm/fado-wm/ana-moura-os-buzios-wm/
Experience the sound of fado.

http://vimeo.com/28961519
Shark diving up-close in the Azores.

Books

Countries Around the World: Portugal by Charlotte Guillain (Raintree, 2012)

Junior Jetsetters Guide to Lisbon by Pedro Marcelino (Junior Jetsetters Inc, 2010)

Countries of the World: Portugal (National Geographic Society, 2009)

Tea please!
Catarina Bragança, a Portuguese lady who married the English King Charles II, is credited for making tea drinking popular in Britain!

Glossary

archipelago A group of islands.

Celts People who lived in Europe in pre-Roman times.

colony A country or area that is ruled by another country.

dictator A ruler with total power over a country, usually obtained by force.

economy The wealth, industry and resources in a country.

empire A group of nations under the power of a single ruler or sovereign country.

export Something that is shipped and sold abroad.

geyser A hot spring that spurts jets of water and steam into the air.

hamlet A small settlement, usually smaller than a village.

monk A religious man who lives alone or in a monastery with other monks.

Moors North African people who conquered southern Portugal in the 700s.

port A strong, sweet type of wine.

republic A country or state without a monarch, usually led by an elected President or Prime Minister.

suburb An area, usually residential, on the outskirts of a city.

textiles The industry involved in making fabrics.

tsunami A huge, destructive tidal wave.

urban Relating to towns or cities, rather than the countryside.

Visigoths Germanic people who invaded the Romans and ruled much of southern France, Spain and Portugal from the 400s to the early 700s.

Index

Unpacked

Australia
Australia: Unpacked
Exploration and Discovery
City Sights
Not All Desert
Aussie Animals
Long Distance Travellers
Go, Aussie, Go!
Mine Time
On the Coast
Native Australians
Aussie Tucker
Everyday Life
Coming to Australia

978 0 7502 7726 6

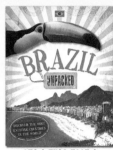

Brazil
Brazil: Unpacked
A World of Faces
Let's Go to Rio!
Viva Futebol!
Jungle Giant
Nature's Treasure Trove
Highways and Skyways
Bright Lights, Big Cities
Life, Brazilian Style
Looking Good
Arts for All
Adventurous Tastes
Prepare to Party!

978 0 7502 7997 0

France
France: Unpacked
The City of Light
Ruling France
Fruit of the Earth
Home and Away
Power and Progress
Grand Designs
Bon Appetit
The Arts
En Vacance
Made in France
Allez Sport
Life in France

978 0 7502 7728 0

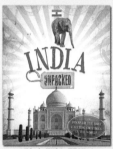

India
India: Unpacked
From 0 to a Billion
Touring India
Everyone's Game
Wild Wonders
Rocks, Rivers, Rains
Life on the Land
High-tech, Low-tech!
Staggering Cities
Everyday India
Spice is Nice
Bollywood Beats
Bright Arts

978 0 7502 7725 9

Italy
Italy: Unpacked
The Romans
Rome: the Eternal City
Way to Go
Food Glorious Food
La Bella Figura
Mountains and Volcanoes
The Italian Arts
Calcio!
North and South
Everyday Life
Super Cities
Italian Inventions

978 0 7502 7727 3

Portugal
Portugal: Unpacked
Small Country, Big Story
Let's Play!
Holiday Hotspot
Sun, Sand and Serras
Island Magic
Charismatic Cities
Made in Portugal!
Country Corkers
Wild Times
Make Yourself at Home
Surf 'n Turf
Creative Culture

978 0 7502 7886 7

South Africa
South Africa: Unpacked
Three Capitals
The Land
Becoming South Africa
SA Sport
Farming
Rainbow Nation
Fabulous Food
Rich and Poor
Wild Life
Mineral Wealth
On the Coast
Holidays and Festivals

978 0 7502 7729 7

Spain
Spain: Unpacked
A World of Their Own
Fiesta Forever
On the Ball
Highlands and Islands
Sleepless Cities
Escape to the Country
Wild Spain
Spanish Life
All You Can Eat
Hola World!
Olé, Olé!
Eye-Popping Arts

978 0 7502 7730 3

WAYLAND
www.waylandbooks.co.uk